TO

_____

FROM

Published by Simple Truths, an imprint of Sourcebooks, Inc.
P.O. Box 4410, Naperville, Illinois 60567-4410
(630) 961-3900
Fax: (630) 961-2168
www.sourcebooks.com

Book Design: Vieceli Design Company, West Dundee, Illinois
Editing by Julie Kellogg
Photography Credit
    Cover
    Corbis — Top left, bottom left and right
    Getty — Top middle and right
    Dan Green Archives—Bottom middle
    Inside
    iStockphoto — 12, 18, 38-39, 48-49, 54, 62, 64, 65, 71, 72, 73, 82, 83, 84, 108, 116
    Getty Images — 22-23, 27, 34, 50, 55, 57, 61, 80,
    Corbis — 24, 28, 30 (2 shots), 36, 37, 40, 41, 44, 47, 52, 53, 58, 88, 89, 90, 96, 104, 110, 112
    Dan Green Archives
    John Baker Archives — 14 (2 shots), 17

www.simpletruths.com

Printed and bound in the United States of America

WOZ 10 9 8 7 6 5 4 3 2

DEDICATION

To my parents for their infinite belief...

To my girls for their constant inspiration...

To my wife for her enduring love...

TABLE OF

CONTENTS

> # "BELIEVE AND ACT AS IF IT WERE IMPOSSIBLE TO FAIL."
>
> — CHARLES F. KETTERING

The words Finish Strong have become a driving force in my life. For more than ten years, they have been my personal mantra for achieving excellence in — life, sport, and business. I have personally embraced the finish strong mindset in all aspects of my life. And, when faced with a challenge or adversity, I remind myself …

"REGARDLESS OF WHAT CAME BEFORE
OR OF WHAT HAS YET TO COME,
WHAT MATTERS MOST RIGHT NOW
IS HOW I CHOOSE TO RESPOND TO
THE CHALLENGE BEFORE ME.
WILL I LIE DOWN OR WILL I FIGHT?
THE CHOICE IS MINE AND I CHOOSE TO
FINISH STRONG."

— DAN GREEN

From this attitude, I have created a personal level of accountability for everything I do. **I don't always get the result I want. But in the times that I have had to lean on my commitment, I always felt a greater sense of accomplishment and satisfaction knowing that I gave it all I had.**

The purpose of this book is to introduce you to the "Finish Strong Attitude" and hope that you will embrace it. The stories I've chosen are amazing examples of people who exemplify the finish strong spirit in sport, business and life. Therefore, my wish for you is to always…Finish Strong.

FS

COURAGE

"*Most of us have far more courage than we ever dreamed we possessed.*"
DALE CARNEGIE

"*Have the courage to live. Anyone can die.*"
ROBERT CODY

"*Courage is almost a contradiction in terms. It means a strong desire to live taking the form of a readiness to die.*"
GILBERT K. CHESTERTON

FEAR IS IN THE
EYE OF THE BEHOLDER

I t was a perfect day for surfing off the coast of Kauai. A 13 year old surfing protégé had just finished riding a twenty foot wave and was lying face down on her surf board. Preparing to paddle out to catch another wave, her thoughts of becoming a professional surfer shifted in an instant. Without warning, she felt a tug on her left arm and in a split second she realized that she'd been attacked by a shark.

As she struggled to gain her composure she realized something even more horrifying – the fourteen foot tiger shark had bitten clean through her board, taking her left arm in a single bite. At that moment in time, survival and not surfing became a priority.

Bethany Hamilton learned to surf at the age of 4. When she was 8, she entered her first contest and won both of the events that she competed in. At the age of 10 she placed 1st in the "11-under girls", 1st in the "15-under girls," and 2nd in the "12-under boys" division at the Volcom Puffer Fish contest. She was determined to become a professional surfer and was certainly on track to make it happen. Then, in one violently swift moment on that fall day in 2003, it seemed her dreams would be shattered.

However, Bethany was born with the heart of a lion and the competitive spirit of a thoroughbred. She was determined to return to the water to surf. Leaning on support from her friends, family and her faith in God, Bethany recovered rapidly and within ten weeks from the attack was surfing again. **Convinced she could overcome her physical challenge, she worked hard to learn to surf around her disability. But she also had to overcome the psychological fear of another attack. Bethany would face her fears by singing and praying when she was out on the water.**

Incredible as it seems, less than a year from her attack, Bethany returned to competition taking fifth place at the National Surfing Championships and first place at the first event for the Hawaii National Scholastic Surfing Association. She was recognized by ESPN in 2004 and received an ESPY award for Best Comeback Athlete of the year.

Bethany's ability to overcome her physical and mental challenges puts her in an elite class of achievers. **She chose to...Finish Strong.**

Her unique ability to confront her fears, embrace them and then continue moving forward in the direction of her goals is the perfect definition of courage.

WHAT'S IN A *NAME*?

John Baker was too short and slight to be a runner for his high school track team. But, John loved to run and he wanted to make the team. His best friend, John Haaland, was a tall and promising runner and heavily recruited by the Manzano High School track coach, but he wanted nothing to do with the sport. John Baker convinced the track coach to let him join the team under the premise that his best friend would follow. The coach agreed and John Baker became a runner.

The team's first meet was a 1.7 mile cross-country race through the foothills of Albuquerque. The reigning state champion, Lloyd Goff, was running and all eyes were on him. The race began and the pack of runners led by Goff disappeared behind the hill. The spectators waited. A minute passed then two and three. Then the silhouette of a single runner appeared. The crowd assumed that it was one of the favorites. But to everyone's amazement, it was John Baker leading the way to the finish line. In his first meet, he blew away the field and set a new meet record.

When asked what happened behind the hill, Baker explained that during the halfway point of the run, he was struggling hard. He asked himself a question:

"Am I doing my best?"

Still unsure if he truly was giving his best effort, he fixed his eyes on the back of the runner in front of him.

"One at a time,"
he thought. His entire focus was on one thing — to pass the runner in front of him.

He committed to himself that nothing would distract him—fatigue, pain, nothing. One by one he caught and passed each runner in front of him until there was no one else to pass.

As the season progressed, John proved that first race was not a fluke. Once the race began, the fun loving, unassuming teenager became a fierce and relentless competitor that refused to lose. By the end of his junior year, John had broken six meet records and was largely regarded to be the best miler in the state. In his senior year he ran the entire track and cross-country season undefeated, winning the state championship in both events. The future certainly looked bright for the seventeen year old.

John entered the University of New Mexico in 1962 and he took his training to the next level by running over ten miles a day. In the spring of 1965, Baker and his team faced the most feared team in track — the University of Southern California Trojans. There

was little doubt that the mile belonged to the Trojans. During the race Baker led for the first lap then purposely slipped back to fourth. At the far turn of the third lap, Baker collided with another runner vying for position. Baker stumbled and struggled to stay on his feet, losing valuable time. **With just under 330 yards to go, Baker dug deep, and living up to his reputation, he blew past the leaders to take the victory by 3 seconds.**

Yes. The future looked even brighter for John Baker. After graduating college, Baker set his sights on the 1972 Olympics. In order to have time to train and also make a living, John took a coaching position at Aspen Elementary in Albuquerque where he had the opportunity to work with kids — something he always wanted to do. **Within a few months, Coach Baker became known as the**

coach who cared. He invested a great deal of time and energy into working with his students as individuals. He was not a critical coach but only demanded what he demanded of himself; that each child give their best effort. The kids responded and loved learning from Coach Baker.

In May 1969, just before his twenty-fifth birthday, John noticed that he was tiring prematurely from his workouts. Two weeks later he developed chest pains and one morning he woke with a painfully swollen groin. He went to see his doctor and they discovered that John had an advanced form of testicular cancer. The only chance John had was to undergo surgery. The operation confirmed the worst case. John's cancer had spread. His doctor believed that he had at best six months to live. A second operation would be required.

I can't even begin to imagine the devastation that John Baker must have felt. How easy it would have been to lie down, quit and feel sorry for himself. In fact, shortly before the second operation, John drove to the mountains and prepared to end his life. He did not want to put his family through the pain. Just before he thought of driving off the cliff, he recalled the faces of his children at Aspen and wondered if they would think that this was the best that Coach Baker could do. This was not the legacy that he wanted to leave behind.

At that moment he decided to rededicate his life to his kids and continue striving to give his best effort. John was not a quitter. He drove home determined to give his best effort for the rest of his life.

In September, after extensive surgery and a summer of treatments, John returned to Aspen where he added a unique program to include handicapped kids within the sports program. He appointed kids as "Coach's Time Keeper" or "Chief Equipment Supervisor." Everyone that wanted to was included. By Thanksgiving, letters from parents were arriving daily at Aspen Elementary in praise of Coach Baker. John created a special award for any child that he thought deserved recognition. He used his own trophies as awards, carefully polishing off his own name. He purchased special fabric with his own money and at night would cut blue ribbons to give as awards.

John refused to take medication to help with his pain because he was afraid of how it would impair his ability to work with his kids. In early 1970 John was asked to help coach a small Albuquerque track club for girls — The Duke City Dashers. By that summer the Dashers were a team to contend with. Baker boldly predicted that they would make it to the AAU finals.

By now, Baker's condition was complicated by the chemotherapy treatments. He could not keep any food down, his health rapidly deteriorated and he struggled to make it to his practices. One October at practice a girl ran up to Coach Baker and shouted,

"Coach, your prediction came true, we're going to the AAU championship next month." Baker was elated and wished for one remaining hope — to live long enough to go along. Unfortunately, it was not to be. A few weeks later, John clutched his abdomen and collapsed. He would not be able to make the trip. Then, at the age of twenty-six on Thanksgiving Day in 1970, John Baker passed away – eighteen months after his first visit to the doctor. He had beaten the odds by twelve months. Two days later, the Duke City Dashers won the AAU championship in St. Louis — "for Coach Baker."

As it stands, that would have been the end of the story. Except, a few days after his funeral, the children at Aspen Elementary began calling their school "John Baker School" and others rapidly adopted this change. A movement began to make the new name official. The Aspen principal referred the matter to the Albuquerque school board. In the spring of 1971, 520 families in the Aspen district voted on the matter. There were 520 votes for the name change and none against. That May, at a ceremony attended by hundreds of Baker's friends, family and kids, Aspen Elementary officially became John Baker Elementary.

Today, John Baker Elementary stands as a testament to a courageous young man who believed in giving his best effort right down to the very end. His legacy continues through the dedicated efforts of the John Baker Foundation. The following poem is used with the permission of his foundation and was written by John five years before he was diagnosed with cancer:

"Many thoughts race through my mind
As I step up to the starting line
Butterflies thru my stomach fly
And as I free that last deep sigh,
I feel that death is drawing near,
But the end of the race I do not fear.
For when the string comes across my breast,
I know it's time for eternal rest.

The gun goes off, the race is run,

And only God knows if I've won.

My family and friends and many more

Can't understand what it was for.

But this "Race To Death" is a final test,

And I'm not afraid, for I've done my best."

— JOHN BAKER

"Faith is believing **what you know ain't so.**"

MARK TWAIN

"The only thing that stands between a person and what they want in life is the will to try it and **the faith to believe it possible.**"

RICH DEVOS

"All things are possible **to him who believes.**"

[MARK 9:23]

AN EXPEDITION IN
FAITH

O n August 1, 1914 Sir Ernest Shackleton set sail with a crew of 28 on an expedition to the Antarctic. The goal of their expedition was to cross the Antarctic on foot —something never done before. Shackleton was a successful and highly respected explorer known for his faith, determination and conviction. He was knighted for his successful exhibition to Antarctica in 1907-09.

In order to recruit his crew of 28 he took applications from 5,000 men. Many believe that he placed the following ad in a London newspaper to attract the applicants.

MEN WANTED: FOR HAZARDOUS JOURNEY. SMALL WAGES, BITTER COLD, LONG MONTHS OF COMPLETE DARKNESS, CONSTANT DANGER, SAFE RETURN DOUBTFUL. HONOUR AND RECOGNITION IN CASE OF SUCCESS.

While there is no evidence that this ad actually ran, it does quite appropriately frame the environment that Shackleton was trying to recruit for.

This expedition was going to be different than any other one that Shackleton had led. Five months into the expedition their ship, the Endurance, became stuck in the heavy ice flows near Antarctica. It was not uncommon for ships to get stuck periodically in the ice flows and Shackleton believed that the ice would eventually recede and free the ship. His focus was on the expedition and he held fast on that course. However, over the next three weeks the ship became solidly frozen in the ice. Attempts to free the ship were futile. At the end of February, 1915, the crew prepared the ship to become their camp for the remainder of winter.

At this point, Shackleton abandoned his primary goal for the expedition and turned his focus towards returning to England. His expedition had become a rescue mission.

By October, eight months after being stuck, the pressure created by the ice finally took its toll on the Endurance. The ship began to come apart and sink, making it uninhabitable. The order to abandon ship was given and the entire crew began to salvage as many supplies as they could. They took the sled dogs, food, gear and three lifeboats and moved their camp to the ice flow next to their sinking ship. The temperatures were brutal, reaching -15°F on average. For the next five months the expedition camped on the ice flow surviving on what little food they had left. In April the ice flow they were camped on began to break apart. Shackleton ordered the crew to take only essential supplies and board the life boats. They fled the disintegrating ice flow and traveled seven days by sea to Elephant Island. Elephant Island was a barren place to be stranded, made up mostly of rock covered snow with temperatures reaching -20°. For the next nine months, under Shackleton's leadership, the broken expedition remained loyal, optimistic, focused and faithful to their leader's belief that they would survive. Ultimately, Shackleton knew that their survival depended upon his ability to reach a whaling outpost that was more than 800 miles across the most treacherous ocean seas in the world. Determined to save his crew, Shackleton set out in one of the lifeboats with five crew members to make the journey. The odds of making it were 1 in 100. Nautical scholars consider this journey by lifeboat to be one of the greatest nautical accomplishments in maritime history. Shackleton successfully made it to the outpost and returned to Elephant Island with a rescue party four months later.

On August 30, 1916 after 22 months of being stranded on a barren rock in sub zero temperatures, the crew of the Endurance was rescued. All twenty eight crew members survived the ordeal and most were quick to credit the strong faith of their leader as the catalyst in their survival.

IT AIN'T OVER
TILL IT'S OVER

G oing into the 2004 Summer Olympics in Athens, expectations were very high for Paul Hamm. **He was the reigning world champion — the first U.S. man to ever win a world all-around title.** No American had ever won the men's all-around gold medal in gymnastics and Paul was expected to change that. The only U.S. gymnast to ever medal was Peter Vidmar in the 1984 Olympics. Paul Hamm seemed destined to at least join Vidmar by winning some sort of medal and the expectations were high that he may even win the all-around title.

> **Hamm started strong in the first three events and held a first place lead in the all-around by .038 points. Then, disaster struck. During his vault performance, he under-rotated and missed his landing, causing him to sit down and nearly fall off the platform.**

His score reflected the "cardinal sin" of gymnastics and after the vault competition was over Hamm found himself in twelfth place. I remember watching the telecast and seeing him sitting on the sidelines with a pale look on his face. It was pretty clear by his reaction that at that point in time he believed he had blown his chance of making history.

But, this is where Paul Hamm demonstrated the difference between mediocrity and greatness. **He decided at that point in time to put his fall behind him and move forward, giving his best effort to finish strong.** His next event was coming up and he was first up. He pulled off a great routine on the parallel bars and nailed his dismount. During the next rotation, a few of the competitors in the 6 – 11 places struggled. His great performance on the parallel bars coupled with the struggles of his competitors helped to move Hamm into fourth place in the all-around with his last and strongest event left to play out — the high bar.

Paul was determined to take advantage of this positive turn of events and make sure that he at least won the bronze medal. He was a master of the high bar and he scripted a highly technical routine in order to have a shot at earning the most points possible. The die was cast as the other competitors had finished their routines. Paul was the last to go.

+.012

As I sat and watched the broadcast I could see Paul pour his heart into his routine — you could feel his energy, focus and determination. When he nailed his dismount it was electrifying and even before his score was revealed, you could see on Paul's face that in his own mind he had won; regardless of the outcome. He came back from a crushing failure on the vault and proved to himself that he could execute beyond failure. And as it turns out, in one of the most dramatic comebacks in all of sports he won the gold medal in the men's all-around by 0.012 points, becoming the first U.S. man to ever win the Olympic title. Talk about finishing strong.

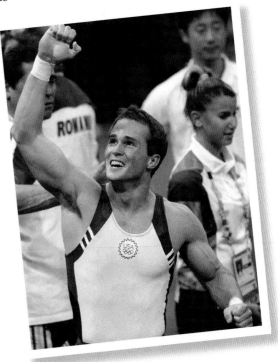

FS

BELIEF

"The will to do springs from the knowledge that we can do."
JAMES ALLEN

"To accomplish great things, we must not only act, but also dream; not only plan, but also believe."
ANATOLE FRANCE

"You'll see it when you believe it."
DR. WAYNE DYER

A SPIRIT
FORGED IN STEEL

On June 23rd, 1940 Wilma Glodean Rudolph was born prematurely and weighed only 4.5 pounds. Wilma became the 20th of 22 children of Ed and Blanche Rudolph. The Rudolph's were African Americans living in a time of segregation. Since the local hospital was for whites only and since the Rudolph's had little money, Mrs. Rudolph was forced to care for Wilma herself. Wilma's early years were very rough. Her mother nursed Wilma through one illness after another — measles, mumps, scarlet fever, chicken pox and double pneumonia. **A few years after her birth, they discovered that Wilma's left leg and foot were not developing normally and that they were becoming deformed.** The doctors told Blanche that Wilma had polio, that she would never walk and that she would have to wear steel braces on her legs. Mrs. Rudolph refused to accept this diagnosis and she set out to find a cure. She discovered that Wilma could receive treatment at Meharry Hospital in Nashville. **For the next two years, Mrs. Rudolph drove Wilma 50 miles each way to get physical therapy.** Eventually, the hospital staff taught Mrs. Rudolph how to do the physical therapy at home. Everyone in the family worked with Wilma, providing her with encouragement to be strong and to get better. Thanks to patience, support, effort and love from her family, at the age of 12, Wilma could walk normally without the assistance of crutches, braces or corrective shoes. She had spent a great deal of her life limited by her illnesses. Wilma felt a freedom that she had never felt. It was then that Wilma decided to become an athlete.

She chose first to pursue basketball just as her older sister did. For three years she rode the bench — not playing a single game. But, Wilma's spirit was forged from steel and she continued to practice hard, refusing to give up. In her sophomore year she became the starting guard for the team and subsequently led the team to a State Championship. But Wilma's first love was to run. **At the age of sixteen (barely four years free of braces) Wilma participated in the 1956 Olympics in track. She won a bronze medal in the 4x100m relay.** However, it was at the state basketball tournament that she was first spotted by Ed Temple, the coach for the women's track team at Tennessee State University. Ed recruited Wilma on a track scholarship and changed the course of her athletic pursuit.

Wilma's most famous athletic achievement was realized at the 1960 Rome Olympics. The little girl that could hardly walk without the assistance of crutches or braces had overcome her challenges and would become the first American woman to win three gold medals in a single Olympics.

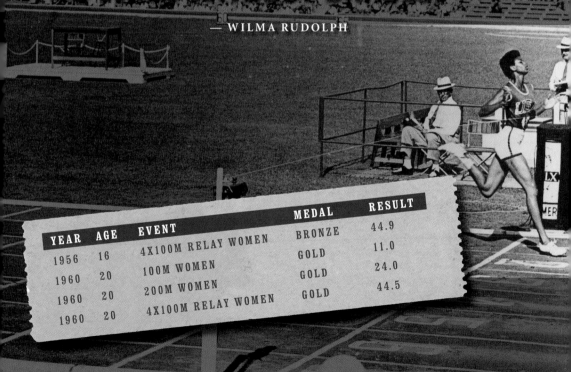

"MY MOTHER TAUGHT ME VERY EARLY TO BELIEVE I COULD ACHIEVE ANY ACCOMPLISHMENT I WANTED TO. THE FIRST WAS TO WALK WITHOUT BRACES."

— WILMA RUDOLPH

YEAR	AGE	EVENT	MEDAL	RESULT
1956	16	4X100M RELAY WOMEN	BRONZE	44.9
1960	20	100M WOMEN	GOLD	11.0
1960	20	200M WOMEN	GOLD	24.0
1960	20	4X100M RELAY WOMEN	GOLD	44.5

FOLLOW THE SUN

Ben was nine years old when his father committed suicide in front of him. It was a horrible thing for a father to do to a son and it had a deep impact on that little boy. Ben would turn to golf as a way to escape the horrors of his childhood. **He was a caddie at a local course in Ft. Worth, TX where he would hit balls after work until dark.** Golf was the perfect game for him as it did not require any interaction with anyone. Ben loved the game and he especially loved the way it felt when he perfectly executed a golf shot. Some days, he would hit so many golf balls that his hands would bleed.

At the age of 17 Ben set his sights on perfecting the game he loved so much and set out on the professional tour. He failed to make it on the tour and was forced to take a full-time job.

HE CONTINUED TO PRACTICE WITH THE BELIEF THAT HE HAD WHAT IT TOOK TO BE A GREAT GOLFER.

A few years later, Ben would make another attempt on the tour. In the process he would meet his wife to be, Valerie. Valerie was an instant inspiration to Ben and she traveled with him from tournament to tournament. In those days, the professional golf tour schedule was coordinated with the places in the country where the sun stayed out the longest. The

11 YEARS
BEFORE
FIRST
PROFESSIONAL WIN

players would "follow the sun" as they traveled from one week to the next. During these early years, Ben would struggle to make a living. On one other occasion he was forced to give up the game for a job with steady income. However, he continued to practice and with the encouragement of his wife he returned to the tour for a third try. In 1940, 11 years after turning pro, Ben Hogan would win his first professional tournament. For the next four years, Ben had modest success on the PGA Tour. However, he had an intense focus and concentration on and off the course. This demeanor projected a cold and unfriendly personality. In fact, it was common for him to walk from shot to shot with his head down staring at his shoe laces. When he did look up, Ben's steely grey eyes and cold stare would instantly intimidate anyone who caught his glance. Ultimately, this look would earn him the nickname...

"THE HAWK"

and the reputation for being an ice-cold and fierce competitor.

In 1944 just as Ben was beginning to achieve success on the tour, he decided to serve his country and he joined the U.S. Air Force. During his service, Ben was limited to how much golf he could play. He would read news articles about the great success of his fellow competitor Byron Nelson. Nelson dominated the PGA Tour during the years that Hogan served in the war. Nelson's record of 11 wins in one year still stands today and will likely never be broken. At the time, the press had anointed Nelson as "Mr. Golf" and "Lord Byron". Hogan was both frustrated and motivated by Byron's success and notoriety. He returned to golf in 1945 determined to establish himself as the dominate player in the game. And he did. **For the next three years Ben would dominate the sport by winning...**

31 events,
2 PGA championships
and the US Open.

In 1949, Ben and Valerie were taking a break from the tour. Driving back to Texas, they ran into a dense fog that forced Ben to slow down to less than ten miles per hour. In a split second, a bus had pulled out to pass a truck and was in the direct path of the Hogan's car. In a selfless act, Ben threw himself in front of Valerie to protect her from the impact. The bus hit them head on, sending the engine into the driver's seat and the steering column into the back seat. Ben would have been killed instantly if he had not tried to protect Valerie. Because of his unselfish courage, Valerie suffered only minor injuries. However, the crash was devastating for Ben and left him clinging to life. He fractured his pelvis, collar bone and left ankle. Blood clots threatened his life and forced the doctors to limit his blood circulation by tying off principal veins in his legs. The doctors said it was unlikely that he would ever walk again, let alone play professional golf. But Ben was a fierce and determined competitor in sport and life. He was determined to overcome the challenges confronting him and with great perseverance and the support of his wife, Ben recovered. He gained enough strength to return to golf in 1950, just eleven months after the accident.

In his first tournament back he forced a playoff with Sam Snead — an amazing accomplishment alone. However, Hogan's physical condition caused him to fade in the play-off and ultimately lose to Snead. Even so, this small success proved to Hogan that he could compete. He continued to practice hard. Today, Hogan is credited with being the first professional golfer to actually "practice". When asked about this he replied. **"You hear stories about me beating my brains out practicing, but ... I was enjoying myself. I couldn't wait to get up in the morning so I could hit balls. When I'm hitting the ball where I want, hard and crisply, it's a joy that very few people experience."** Five months later he would win the U.S. Open, reinforcing his belief in himself. After the accident, Ben's legs were never the same. He could hardly walk eighteen holes without collapsing. Due to this poor condition he could only play seven tournaments each year. However, for the next three years, Ben Hogan would dominate every tournament he entered. During this time, he won 13 of the tournaments that he entered including 6 majors. In 1953, he only entered 6 tournaments but won 5 of them including 3 majors. Winning 3 majors in a single year was a record that would stand for almost fifty years until 2000, when Tiger Woods accomplished the same feat.

64 VICTORIES

Ben Hogan would ultimately retire with
64 professional victories and 9 major titles –
6 of which came after the car crash. He is known today as
the father of the modern golf swing and
Tiger Woods and Jack Nicklaus consider him to be the
best ball striker the game has ever seen.

One of his greatest contributions to the game
is the concept of

"practice."

Before Hogan, the idea of practicing the game of golf
did not exist. His work ethic and commitment to improvement
is the model for today's touring professional.

Ben Hogan overcame a dark childhood memory, early failure at the game of golf and a debilitating car crash to become one of the legends of the game. He continued to be an ambassador of the game and charitable organizations long after his retirement. **Throughout his life, there were many reasons for Ben Hogan to have simply been finished; instead he chose to persevere, to fight and to ultimately finish strong.**

BELIEVE IN MIRACLES

It was 1980 and the US economy was in a recession. Iran had taken Americans hostage and the Russians had invaded Afghanistan. With the cold war in full force, President Carter threatened to boycott the summer Olympics in Moscow in protest of Russia's actions in Afghanistan. Across America, the events of the time were driving **American pride and morale to an all time low point in history. But a hockey game was about to change all of that.**

In the 1980 Winter Olympics at Lake Placid, the USA hockey team was represented by a collection of young college kids, some with pro hockey aspirations. Under the guidance of their coach, Herb Brooks, the young American athletes became a fast, well conditioned and cohesive team. While some viewed Brooks' coaching methods as somewhat questionable, they did result in the development of a physically and mentally tough young hockey team.

Brooks knew how dangerous his team could be. **He also knew that many of their competitors were underestimating his team's potential and had mostly written them off as a medal contender.** Brooks would use this miscalculation to his team's advantage.

In order to make it to the medal round, the USA team had to fight hard in each match. In the opening game against Sweden, they scored with 27 seconds remaining to force a 2-2 tie. This was a significant event for the USA team because the Americans had not beaten the Swedes since 1960. The tie lifted the team's morale and planted that first seed of "belief." Next, the Americans dominated a strong Czech team by winning 7-3 — with seven different Americans scoring. Again, this was another significant event for the young team to take and build upon because the Czechs were largely believed to be a lock for the Silver medal. The USA team would continue their way through the bracket by winning their next three games, ultimately positioning them for the first medal round against the Russians.

Belief had turned into passion for the Americans.

The young USA team had been given essentially no chance at beating the stronger Russian team. The Russians had dominated Olympic hockey for years and their players were considered to be professionals by all accounts because of the strength of the European hockey league and the financial backing of the Soviet Union. The Soviets took great pride in their dominance. In fact, just before the start of the Olympics, they crushed the young American team 10-3 in an exhibition match at Madison Square Garden. It was a humiliating loss in front of the American fans, and it seemed clear that the Russians were destined for gold.

Fast-forward a few weeks and the USA team finds themselves up against the Soviets in the first medal round, battling not only for a medal, but also for the pride of America. The tensions between Russia and The United States were very high and this hockey game took on greater meaning for both nations.

The Russians started strong and took a 2-1 lead early in the first period. **With the final seconds winding down in the first period, the Russians made a critical mistake.** Thinking that the period was almost over, they backed-off and began skating off the ice. In fact, there was just enough time for USA's Mark Johnson to take a rebounded shot with 1 second left and drill it into the Russian's net. The USA had tied the game 2-2. The Russians would score quickly again in the second period and again the Americans would answer resulting in a 3-3 tie going into the third period. The Russians had thrown everything they had at the Americans and the young team answered at each blow. Now, the Americans no longer believed that they could beat the Russians; they KNEW they could. Midway through the third period, Mike Euruzione, the team captain, would catch the puck and fire it past the Russian goaltender to give the Americans a 4-3 lead with ten minutes remaining. The field house erupted and the energy level went through the roof. Could they actually pull this off? Ten minutes would seem like an eternity. **Team USA would need to finish strong** to hold off the Russian assault. And the Russians fought hard, firing ten shots for every one shot made by the USA team. The level of emotion and energy in the rink was beyond anything you could imagine. **As the time wound down, the American fans began the chant U-S-A, U-S-A. This was not about a hockey game. It was about American pride.** The well-conditioned USA team held off the Russians and won. They finished strong in what became known as the **Miracle on Ice.**

Today, almost 30 years later, most people believe that this unlikely victory resulted in a gold medal for the USA. It did not. The win over the Russians put team USA through to the next round where they would later defeat Finland to win the gold. In six of seven games played, the USA team had to come back from a deficit to win. They truly embodied the spirit of belief, persistence and passion. And, they definitely finished strong!

"Do you believe in miracles?"

— AL MICHAELS, *Sports broadcaster His famous call as time ran out in the game*

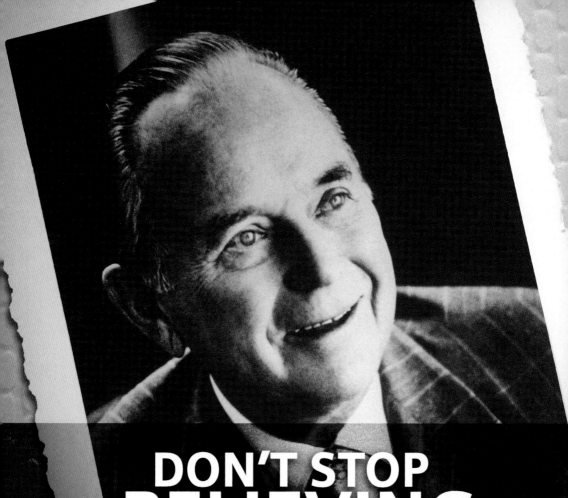

DON'T STOP
BELIEVING

R ay Kroc, the founder of McDonald's, is a great example of how to Finish Strong. Today, every five hours somewhere around the world a new McDonald's restaurant is opening. However, what's amazing about McDonald's is that Ray did not conceive the idea until he was 52 years old. By that time he had already been a struggling paper cup salesman, real estate broker, piano player and milk shake mixer. Here's what Ray said about that time in his life:

"I was 52 years old. I had diabetes and incipient arthritis. I had lost my gall bladder and most of my thyroid gland in earlier campaigns, but I was convinced that the best was ahead of me."

— RAY KROC

47 MILLION
117 COUNTRIES

He deeply believed that this new restaurant concept was his biggest idea ever. He chose to fully commit himself to make it happen. However, in order to realize his dream he would have to mortgage his home and borrow heavily. You have to remember that Kroc conceived the idea in a time when the family home-dining experience was very much ingrained in our culture. People did not eat out very often. However, Ray believed if Americans could order good food in a clean place and get it fast, they would come. And, of course, he was right.

He truly was the father of "fast food."

Most of us at 52 years old would find every reason not to take the risk and roll the dice on an untested concept. However, Ray believed in himself and was determined to succeed. Today because of Ray Kroc living his dream, McDonald's serves more than 47 million customers a day across 117 different countries and employs hundreds of thousands around the world. He once said, "When you find something that you love to do, you'll never have to work another day of your life." He took the risk and finished strong.

FS

ATTITUDE

"Life is *10* percent what you make it
and *90* percent how you take it."

IRVING BERLIN

"How you respond to the challenge
in the second half will determine what you
become after the game, whether you are
a winner or loser."

LOU HOLTZ

KEEP *CLIP'N* ALONG

By embracing the attitude to Finish Strong, I've created a personal level of accountability that goes with me wherever I go. The first time I really discovered the power of this mindset was early in my selling career. In the early nineties I sold software systems to commercial banks. A great deal of my selling efforts involved prospecting for leads over the phone. No matter how good you are at selling over the phone, it can be challenging to push yourself to make one more call — and a key to success in selling is "making one more call."

As a method of daily goal setting, I would start my day in the office by taking out twenty five paper clips from my desktop paper clip holder. I would place the paper clips on a coaster right next to the holder which was next to the phone.

Each time I engaged in a meaningful selling conversation I would take one of the paper clips from the pile and put it back in the holder. **I knew that if I created twenty five selling conversations each day, that my ultimate sales goals would be reached.** I made a commitment not to leave the office until every paper clip was put back. There were many times when the day was over for everyone else and I had one paperclip sitting on that coaster staring at me. In order to finish strong, I needed to have one more selling conversation. I dialed until I succeeded. I never left a paperclip sitting on the coaster and I never put one back that I did not earn. The level of activity I created during this time stuffed my sales pipeline with opportunities.

My career took off and I tripled my income in the course of two years — all because I chose to FINISH STRONG.

"THE MOST IMPORTANT THING ABOUT GOALS IS HAVING ONE..."

— GEOFFREY ABERT

TO FINISH *FIRST*
YOU MUST FIRST FINISH

Because of the success I achieved in sales, I had the good fortune to pursue another passion of mine — motorsports. **I had a dream to race at the Indy 500 — I like to dream big.** Living in Indianapolis at the time, I was overexposed to the world of motorsports. It was intoxicating. So, I went to racing school to learn to drive open-wheel racecars. After spending a year racing in the Skip Barber race series, a racing friend of mine (who actually did try to qualify for Indy) took me under his wing. His brother owned a race team in Texas and I signed up to race one of his formula fords in the Sports Car Club of America series (SCCA). **My first race was in October of 1993 at Gateway International in St. Louis, MO.** As the race started, I was able to hang with the leaders for the first quarter of the race. They were a bit quicker than me and by the midpoint they had pulled into a half lap lead. I became a bit frustrated and began pushing the limits of my car in an effort to catch them. As a result, I pushed my car deep into a corner and lost control, spinning out and losing valuable time. Fortunately I was able to quickly get back on track but it seemed unlikely that I could catch the leaders.

I was devastated by my mistake — winning seemed out of reach.

Sitting in my cockpit speeding down the backstretch with the cars behind quickly catching up, I had a decision to make. Did I get down on myself and "coast" around the final laps in despair? Or did I pull my belts tight, put my nose down and set a new realistic goal? I drew upon my commitment to finish strong and decided to try to turn the fastest lap of the race. **I remember saying out loud, "Come on Dan, Finish Strong."** I took control of my emotions and got it going. My vision became clear, everything slowed down around me and my focus became intense. On the next to final lap, I passed two cars ahead of me. Coming out of the last turn with one lap to go I could barely see the two leaders at the end of the front stretch diving into turn one. **As I came through turn one, I was shocked to see that the number one and two cars ahead of me had crashed and taken themselves out of the race. I couldn't believe it.** Coming out of the last turn I saw the checkered flag waving. I won! I was shocked. Had I given up after my spin I would never have caught and passed the two cars in front of me and put myself in a position to win. By choosing to finish strong I ended up winning the first SCCA race I entered. **In racing they say that in order to finish first you must first finish. True, but finishing strong is even better.**

"SUCCESS SEEMS TO BE CONNECTED WITH **ACTION.** SUCCESSFUL PEOPLE KEEP MOVING. THEY MAKE MISTAKES, BUT THEY **DON'T QUIT.**"

— CONRAD HILTON

FOCUS ON
PRIORITIES

Through the years, choosing to finish strong has provided me with many benefits: reaching goals, winning a race and gaining satisfaction from knowing I gave it my all. By drawing upon my commitment, I have begun learning to enjoy the ride of life. However, one of the greatest benefits that I've received from this mindset involves my family. A great example of how this attitude has helped me relates to my relationship with my two daughters. A regular part of our night-time routine is to read a story and say our prayers. Sometimes of course, I'm worn out from my day's work or I'm thinking about other things that need to be done. In these times, it can be tempting to try to skip the ritual with my daughters — but I know this would be a mistake. I remind myself of my commitment to finish strong and to focus on my true priorities in life. Because as the quote says: "To the world you may be just one person... but to one person you may be the world".

The cost of regret far exceeds the price of discipline.

FS
COMMITMENT

"**Don't be afraid** to take a big step if
one is indicated. You can't cross a chasm
in two small jumps."
DAVID LLOYD GEORGE

"**The difference between** involvement and
commitment is like ham and eggs. The chicken
is involved; the pig is committed."
MARTINA NAVRATILOVA

"**Keep on going, and the** chances are that you
will stumble on something, perhaps when you
are least expecting it. I never heard of anyone
ever stumbling on something sitting down."
CHARLES KETTERING

DYING TO MAKE A DIFFERENCE

A fter a two year battle with cancer, teenager Miles Levin, unfortunately lost his fight. However, during his final years, he achieved a level of self-awareness, courage and wisdom that most of us will never reach. Miles chose to post his observations on a carepages.com blog and through his writings he inspired thousands of people. He wrote with amazing grace and eloquence. Some of his posts were short:

> "Dying is not what scares me.
> It's dying having no impact."

Some were long and philosophical. But each post served a significant purpose in that it challenged the reader to think more deeply about life, death and making a difference. Through his expressions Miles left this world a better place than he came into it. I can only hope that I do the same with my life. Here's what Miles said just one month after being diagnosed with terminal cancer:

I went to the driving range the other day and I was thinking...
I was thinking how you start out with a big bucket full of golf balls,
and you just start hitting away carelessly. You have dozens of
them, each individual ball means nothing to you so just hit, hit, hit.
One ball gone is practically inconsequential when subtracted from
your bottomless bucket. There are no practice swings or technique
re-evaluations after a bad shot, because so many more tries remain.
Yet eventually you start to have to reach down towards the bottom
of the bucket to scavenge for another shot and you realize that tries
are running out. Now with just a handful left, each swing becomes
more meaningful. The right technique becomes more crucial, so
between each shot you take a couple practice swings and a few
deep breaths. There is a very strong need to end on a good note,
even if every preceding shot was terrible, getting it right at the end
means a lot. You know as you tee up your last ball, "This is my final
shot, I want to crush this with perfection; I must make this count."
Limited quantities or limited time brings a new, precious value and
significance to anything you do. Live every day shooting as if it's
your last shot, I know I have to.

— Miles Alpern Levin, July 7, 2005

"I have tried my best to show what it is to *persevere*, and what it means to be **strong.**"

— MILES LEVIN

Like Miles suggested, we should treat each day as a precious ball of life. Take your time, take a breath and make a practice swing. Make each shot count and most of all finish strong!

OVERNIGHT
SUCCESS

Finishing strong in life, sport or business does not always involve overcoming a challenge in a moment in time. When you live the attitude, it becomes part of you and part of your life. In some cases you will find strength to finish strong in a blink of an eye. For example, you may get an extra burst of energy to finish the last repetition in an exercise. Other times it will fuel you through a project that may take months. However, sometimes it can take a lifetime to realize the benefits of your commitment to Finish Strong. A man named William is testimony to this.

"Harriet Beecher Stowe praised him in the pages of Uncle Tom's Cabin," writes historian and biographer Kevin Belmonte.

> "Novelist E.M. Forester compared him to Gandhi. Abraham Lincoln invoked his memory in a celebrated speech. In the houses of Parliament, Nelson Mandela recalled his tireless labors on behalf of the sons and daughters of Africa, calling Britain 'the land of William Wilberforce – who dared to stand up to demand that the slaves in our country should be freed.'"

It was in 1787 that Wilberforce first became leader of the parliamentary campaign of the Committee for the Abolition of the Slave Trade. In May of 1789, he made his first

House of Commons

163 NAY

88 YEA

major speech on the subject of abolition in the House of Commons. However, getting people to listen was only a small first step. In April of 1791, Wilberforce introduced the first Parliamentary Bill to abolish the slave trade, which was easily defeated by 163 votes to 88. **Six subsequent attempts to pass the bill also failed, the last in 1805. Like any great leader, Wilberforce had cast his vision clearly and often but the outcome had not yet been reached. Still he persisted.**

Two years later, the bill came before Parliament again with a different result. In March of 1807, the Slave Trade Act was passed, abolishing the slave trade from the British Empire.

It was a momentous victory, yet, not the ultimate objective that Wilberforce sought. He continued his campaign for the emancipation of all slaves. Finally, on July 26, 1833 — over forty-five years after setting out — Wilberforce received news that the bill for the abolition of slavery had passed its third reading in the House of Commons. He died three days later but the momentum he created saw his vision through. One month after his death, Parliament passed the Slavery Abolition Act giving all slaves in the British Empire their freedom.

"Have the dogged determination to follow through to achieve your goal: Regardless of circumstances or whatever other people say, think or do."

— PAUL J. MEYER

FS

PURPOSE

"*Nothing changes until something moves.*"
UNKNOWN

"*It doesn't matter where you've been, it only matters where you are going.*"
BRIAN TRACY

"*The secret to success is consistency of purpose.*"
BENJAMIN DISRAELI

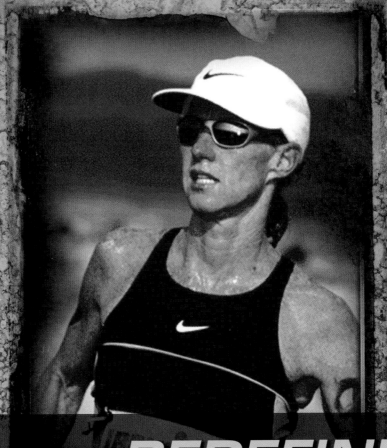

REDEFINE
YOUR LIMITS

ABC sports called it one of the most defining moments in sports. After leading the 1982 Kona, HI Triathlon for more than 7 hours, Julie Moss collapsed fifty feet from the finish line. Millions of television viewers painfully watched Julie stagger then fall, stagger then fall and stagger then crawl across the finish line. What they did not see was the mental transformation that took place within Julie during that time. This was a defining moment in her life.

Julie was a 23-year-old student participating in her first triathlon largely in part to do research for her exercise physiology thesis. She entered the event because she believed it would provide her with valuable experience to incorporate into her thesis. She did not consider herself to be an exceptional athlete and later explained, "I used to dread getting called onto the court for volleyball or having to serve in tennis," she says of her high school sporting days.

"I really wasn't ready for the pressure of leading the race."

50 YARDS

But leading an Ironman race can have a powerful effect on people and Julie experienced that first hand. During the mid point of the run portion — the final leg — her desire to simply finish began to evolve into a desire to finish fast and finish first. Never in her entire life had she experienced that competitive side to her psyche. However, she was about to experience the effects of her poor diet and hydration during the race. At that time, very little was understood about nutrition, hydration and high performance activity. The Power Bar wasn't invented yet and most athletes believed that bananas and water were the nutritional staples of high performance — we know differently today. Julie began to feel the effects of poor nutrition and hydration during the event. With about seven miles to go she was forced to add intervals of walking then running. Her body was shutting down, but her mind was not. **"It took all my focus just to keep my body working," she recalled.** "The image was that I was pretty out of it, but it was taking all my focus just to keep going. I had to concentrate so much on how I placed my foot on the ground. If I was off by a bit, my leg would just buckle."

TO FINISH

With 100 yards to go, Julie's mind began to play tricks on her. She imagined herself running across the finish line and kept trying to run instead of walk to the finish. Later she said that she probably would have won the race if she simply decided to walk instead of run. So for the last 50 yards she continued to fall, rise, step and fall over and over again. It was painful to watch. Julie was on her hands and knees within feet of the finish line when the second place runner passed Julie to win the race. A few seconds later, Julie crawled across the finish line — creating one of the most dramatic finishes in sports history. For Julie, it was much more than a generic defining moment in sports; this was her defining moment.

At some point in everyone's life we all have a defining moment. Julie's just happened to be captured on film and in front of millions of people. She tapped an inner strength that she never knew she possessed and rose above the physical and mental adversity confronting her to achieve her goal. For Julie, this moment in time shifted the course of her life by redefining her physical and mental personal limits.

CAPITALIZE
ON CATASTROPHE

The story of Jim J. Braddock, the "Cinderella Man," is one of my favorites. It's about a working man's rise to the top, his fall to the very bottom and then his ascension to heights he never imagined. And through it all he discovered the true meaning of life.

Jim Braddock spent the better part of the 1920's boxing in the light heavyweight division. During this time, he gained a reputation for being a fierce competitor with a right hand punch that could stop a bulldozer. His rise through the professional ranks began in 1926. He won most of his fights and earned a respectable reputation and living. By all accounts Jim Braddock was a successful man with a good life.

Jim's first big shot came on a warm summer night in 1929. He would face Tommy Loughran for the light heavyweight championship of the world. Loughran was a young and bright fighter who knew how dangerous Braddock's right hand could be. He studied Braddock's style and went into the fight with a strategy to avoid the right hand. His research paid off and Braddock was never able to land a solid punch with his right. The fight went fifteen rounds and Braddock lost the decision to Loughran. Braddock took this loss very hard.

With this loss, everything Braddock had worked to achieve seemed to be gone. But little did he know how much harder things would get. Less than two months after the loss to Loughran on September 3, 1929, the stock market crashed and thrust America into the Great Depression.

6-22
AFTER LOUHRAN LOSS

Like millions of Americans, Jim Braddock lost everything with the crash. With no work available, Jim continued to box in order to provide for his family. Unfortunately, Jim's boxing career hit the skids during this time. He lost sixteen of twenty two fights. To make matters worse, he shattered his powerful right hand and lost his greatest boxing asset. Under pressure to support his family, Jim quit boxing and filed for government relief. For the next few years, Jim would struggle to make ends meet. He worked odd jobs on the docks and took whatever other work he could find. **His family finances grew worse and at times they had very little food or heat for their apartment. It was during these years that Jim Braddock discovered how important his family was to him. Because of this emotional time in his life, Jim would rediscover the true meaning of winning.**

A favorite saying of mine is that "God's timing is never early and never late." This was true for Jim Braddock in 1934. Due to a last minute cancellation and the dogged determination of his manager, Jim was given the opportunity to fight on the undercard for the heavyweight championship bout between Max Baer and Primo Carnera at Madison Square Garden. However, there were compelling reasons for him not to take the fight. For one, the fight was at the heavyweight class and Braddock was not a heavyweight fighter. In fact, he was almost forty pounds lighter than the average heavyweight. Also, his right hand was not the same as before and he was uncertain if it would hold up under the stress. And finally, he had not been training for the fight. None of this mattered to Jim. To him, this was an opportunity to make some money to improve his family's well being. **As slight a chance as it was, Jim believed he could win and that meant a better future for his family. Winning now meant so much more than it did before.** With no training and a bum right hand, Braddock would shock the boxing community by knocking out John Griffin in the third round. Jim later said that his time spent working on the docks had kept him in shape and also helped him to develop a strong left hook – which no one expected.

As word spread of the upset, Braddock's popularity grew and the fight promoters would leverage this popularity to their advantage. As a result, he was given a shot at

John Henry Lewis, a fighter that had previously beaten Jim. For this fight Jim was a huge underdog. Yet again, Jim delivered with a tenth round victory. In doing so, **Jim Braddock became an inspiration to the nation during a time that desperately needed something to cheer about.** Millions of Americans related to Jim and his working man's story.

In the spring of 1935, Braddock was matched up against Art Lasky. Lasky was the number one contender to fight Max Baer, the reigning heavyweight champion. At the time, there were no discussions about Braddock getting a shot at Baer because nobody believed he could beat Lasky. The fight promoters viewed this fight mostly as a way to capitalize on Braddock's popularity and to make a buck off of him — **Braddock winning just did not seem like an option.** Jim took Lasky to fifteen rounds. In doing so he punished Lasky so much that he won a unanimous decision. With this victory, he became the number one contender to fight Max Baer for the heavyweight championship of the world — less than a year after working on the docks. The Cinderella Man was born.

Braddock faced Max Baer on June 13, 1935 at Madison Square Garden. He entered the ring a 10-1 underdog and gave up over 20 pounds in weight to Baer. Baer was a ferocious fighter with a hammering right hand who had previously killed two other fighters in the ring. Braddock learned a valuable lesson from his earlier loss to Tommy

Loughran. He studied Baer's fight footage and identified a strategy to avoid Baer's crushing right hand — just as Loughran had done to him. **In one of the greatest upsets in all sports history, the Cinderella Man battled Baer for fifteen rounds winning a unanimous decision to become the heavyweight champion of the world.**

15 ROUNDS
BRADDOCK VS. BAER

In less than a year, Jim Braddock turned his life completely around. Through his personal trials, he was able to redefine the meaning of his life and thus tap an inner strength greater than he ever knew he had. It was this new strength that empowered him to achieve his goals. When presented the opportunity to make a comeback, the shift he made mentally had prepared him for the fight better than any physical training could have done. Jim's new outlook on life lived on past his boxing career and he would go on to lead a successful and prosperous life until his death in 1974.

DISCIPLINE

> *"Great beginnings are not as important as the way one finishes."*
>
> DR. JAMES DOBSON

> *"Nothing will work unless you do."*
>
> JOHN WOODEN

> *"What it lies in our power to do, it lies in our power not to do."*
>
> ARISTOTLE

KM

DON'T LET LIFE
PIN YOU DOWN

Kyle Maynard is a regular guy with a love to compete. He knows that to truly live you must set your sights on a goal and never give up. The fire that burns in his belly helped propel him to contend for the Georgia state high school wrestling championship in 2004. Not such a big deal you might say — except for the remarkable fact that Kyle has no arms or legs. He was born a congenital amputee — his arms ending at his elbows, his legs at his knees.

> **The first time I saw Kyle on an ESPN special** (he won an ESPY award for the Best Athlete with A Disability in 2004) **I was immediately struck by how normal he seemed. During the special, they showed Kyle doing all of the things that any other person or athlete would do.**

He spoke with passion and conviction and he never left me with the impression that the world owed him anything. I was amazed to see him training hard, lifting weights — he has cannon balls for shoulders. Using a specially designed attachment, he was pushing more than double his own body weight. I was instantly inspired to learn more about this amazing person.

From the beginning, Kyle's parents, Anita and Scott, were determined to raise a normal child. They insisted that he learned to feed himself and play with the other kids like any other child would do.

When Kyle saw other kids picking up crayons with their fingers, he learned to pick them up by using the crease in his short, but sensitive biceps.

His grandmother Betty was a source of inspiration and would often take him to the grocery store where she would instill a sense of confidence by encouraging Kyle to sit up and look folks in the eye and smile. He was fitted with prosthetic devices at a young age, but quickly dismissed them because they were too restrictive. He wanted to be free to run and play just like the other kids and those devices kept him from doing so.

Kyle led an active childhood. He played street hockey with his friends (he was the goalie) and in sixth grade was able to make the football team. Kyle hung tough on the football team, but his physical differences put him at a disadvantage against other players. Eventually, his father encouraged him to try another sport that would pit Kyle on an even plane with his competition — wrestling.

KYLE MAYNARD

0 - 35

RECORD THROUGH HIS FIRST 35 MATCHES

Kyle started wrestling in sixth grade. He lost his first 35 matches in a row. During this period of time, Kyle had to dig deep to find the confidence to continue. Kyle however, was a warrior and he didn't like to lose. With the support of his father, a former wrestler, he learned to train with weights, became very strong and learned some moves unique to his strengths. Kyle overcame the self-doubt he felt during his early wrestling days and became a winner. In his senior year, Kyle won 35 times on the varsity squad and qualified for the state championship. In the state tournament, Kyle won his first three matches and had to face his final opponent with a broken nose. Although Kyle did not win the state championship, he gained a level of self-confidence and became a source of inspiration for everyone that he met.

Kyle graduated high school and attends the University of Georgia, where he continues to wrestle and inspire others. As a member of the Washington Speaker's Bureau, Kyle is regularly asked to give motivational talks. But what he has to say has little to do with his perceived physical differences. Rather, he talks of overcoming fear and doubt and what it takes to compete and win — just as any other champion would do. To this day, Kyle has never been pinned by an opponent. What a fitting metaphor for his life.

"IT'S NOT WHAT HAPPENS TO YOU, BUT HOW YOU REACT TO IT THAT MATTERS."

— EPICTETUS

I n stark contrast to many of the athletic endeavors featured in this book, the story of Helen Keller is one that also exemplifies the finish strong spirit — overcoming great adversity to achieve success.

Helen was born in 1880 into an affluent southern family in Alabama. At the age of nineteen months, Helen was stricken ill and left deaf and blind. I can remember when my daughters were that age. They were alive, aware, vibrant, happy and engaging. Can you imagine the fear that little girl must have felt when her world went dark? In fact, as the years progressed, Helen became wild and hard to control. If it were not for her young friend Martha Washington, the daughter of one of the Keller family's servants, Helen may have been put into a sanitarium to live out her life in complete darkness. However, Martha befriended Helen and taught her to communicate through sign language. **She taught Helen over sixty different signs that helped her communicate with her family. Most of us think of Annie Sullivan as the "miracle worker", when in fact it was young Martha that truly helped Helen's world open up.** Experts agree that Martha's help was critical to Helen's later success. It's ironic that because of her limited communication she became demanding, spoiled and uncontrollable. When she was six, Helen's mother reached out to friends to find help for Helen. She was referred to a specialist working with deaf children

— Alexander Graham Bell. Mr. Bell spent time with Helen and ended up referring her to the Perkins Institute for the Blind. And this is where she met Annie Sullivan.

Annie was a twenty year old graduate of the school and was partially blind. She had been completely blind, but through a series of operations recovered part of her sight. Annie understood Helen's world. She received permission to take Helen away from her family to help her focus. After taking Helen into seclusion and isolating her from her family, she was able to essentially break her of her tantrums and ill behavior. Under Annie's guidance, Helen's world would open up exponentially. Her sight and sound limitations became great strengths and provided her with great wisdom. She once said,

"What I am looking for is not out there, it is in me."

She would go on to become the first blind person to ever graduate from college. She traveled the world as a famous speaker and author. She is remembered as an advocate for people with disabilities amid numerous other causes. In 1915, she founded Helen Keller International, a non-profit organization for preventing blindness. In 1920, she helped to found the American Civil Liberties Union (ACLU). Keller and Sullivan became very close friends and they traveled the world together meeting international dignitaries from more than 40 countries. She also met some amazing people along her journey. She met every

US President from Grover Cleveland to Lyndon B. Johnson and was friends with many famous figures, including Alexander Graham Bell, Charlie Chaplin and Mark Twain. Helen passed away in 1968 at the age of 87.

I have to ask, how could a deaf and blind little six year old in the 1800's rise to such prominence and make such a difference in the world? Without question her mother, Martha Washington and Annie Sullivan have to be given a great deal of credit. But, I believe that the foundation for her success stemmed from within the spirit of Helen herself. Without the deep-seeded desire to learn and to rise above the challenges before her, she could not have overcome her physical limitations regardless of how much help she had. At the end of the day, we must all eventually look inward to grow outward. **Helen understood this better than most. Like many of the people in this book, in her own way Helen Keller was a champion who clearly finished strong.**

"We don't see things as they are; we see things as we are."

—ANAIS NIN

RISK

"Play the game for more than you can afford to lose...only then will you learn the game."

WINSTON CHURCHILL

"People who take risks are the people you'll lose against."

JOHN SCULLEY

"Only those who will risk going too far can possibly find out how far they can go."

T.S. ELIOT

LIVE WITH NO
REGRETS

I was a freshman at Oklahoma State in 1983 when the Nebraska Cornhuskers came to town to play our Cowboys. The Cornhuskers had dominated all of their opponents when they came to Stillwater and were the number one ranked team in college football.

They opened their season by crushing Penn State, the defending national champions, 44 – 6. Prior to coming to Stillwater they had outscored their opponents 289 to 56.

I remember the game like it was yesterday because we gave them their first and only real scare that year — losing 14 -10. It was a heartbreaking loss for us. However, it was also very memorable because of the great players I got to see. Mike Rozier would go on to win the Heisman Trophy that year, Turner Gill was an absolute wizard to watch at QB and wide receiver Irving Fryar would ultimately become the number one draft pick in the NFL.

In 1983, the head coach for Nebraska was Tom Osborne. He had never won a national championship and was under tremendous pressure to do so, but by all accounts he was on his way to bringing Nebraska their first championship. His offense was probably the greatest college offense ever to take the field.

They finished their season with a perfect record and would enter the Orange Bowl as the number one ranked team in the country.

They would face the Miami Hurricanes. The Hurricanes entered their season unranked and were slaughtered in their opener by number seven ranked Florida. That would be their first and only loss of the season. After their first loss, the Hurricanes dominated every game they played. As a result, they entered the Orange Bowl as the fourth ranked team.

Two key games had been decided prior to the Orange Bowl. The number two ranked Texas Longhorns were upset in the Cotton Bowl by number three ranked Georgia and the Auburn Tigers put away Michigan in the Sugar Bowl. Because of these events, the Orange Bowl would be played for the national title.

As you can imagine, the game was hyped by the media as the game of the century. **Could the previously unknown Hurricanes actually win? Would Tom Osborne get his first national title? Could the Nebraska offense be stopped?** The game lived up to the hype. It was an emotional roller-coaster to watch and would take too many pages to fully recap. But, the simple truth is this: with 1:46 left to play in the game the Cornhuskers had the ball on Miami's 26 yard line with fourth down and eight to go. They were trailing Miami 31-24. In one of the greatest plays in college football history, Turner Gill ran the option to the right, pitched the ball to Jeff Smith who ran it in for a touchdown and pulled the Cornhuskers within 1 point with under a minute left to play. **They could tie the game with an extra point or they could win outright with a two point conversion.** Since there was no overtime to decide an outright winner, a tie game would leave the championship to be decided by the coaches and media polls. But, an outright win would seal the championship for the Huskers.

What happened next perfectly defines the meaning of risk. Tom Osborne put the championship on the line and went for two points and the win. He had the best run offense in the country and was completely confident that they could pull it off. He also knew that Miami would be expecting the run. So, instead of using his bread-and-butter run offense he opted to pass the ball. Gill's pass fell incomplete and after a failed onside kick attempt, Nebraska lost their first game of the year and the national championship.

The next morning football fans across the country debated the "go-for-two" call. Many argued that given a tie, Nebraska would have easily won the vote for the title. Osborne and his team had a different perspective. They wanted to finish strong and win the game and the championship outright. They took the path that they believed would get them there. **It was a calculated risk that Osborne never second guessed. In this instance it didn't work, but they gave it their best shot and to this day he does not regret it.**

"NOBODY WHO EVER GAVE HIS BEST REGRETTED IT!"

— GEORGE HALAS

BEGINNINGS

This is the last chapter in my book, and I'll bet that you've noticed an emerging theme throughout. **For most of the champions, their great accomplishment was not the end of their greatness; rather it was the beginning of greater things to come.** Each used their moment in time to propel them forward in life.

Bethany Hamilton would survive the shark attack to become a world-class surfer and become an inspiration to thousands of people around the world. After he achieved his success in boxing, Jim Braddock repaid the government aid money that he was given during his hard times and went on to live a full and prosperous life. John Baker's commitment to give his best effort lives on at the elementary school bearing his name. After her Olympic glory, Wilma Rudolph would champion civil rights causes and inspire thousands of children as a teacher. Ray Kroc's belief in himself would ultimately lead to the creation of the Ronald McDonald House charity — a place dedicated to helping cancer victims and their families find peace during difficult times.

The Finish Strong attitude is grounded in the principle that you never "get there" in life and that you should always keep moving forward. I love the way that John Naber, the four-time gold medal winning Olympic swimming champion, characterizes his achievement. When asked if winning four Olympic gold medals was the highlight of his life, he replied, "I hope not. I've still got a lot of living left to do and I hope that my greatest achievement is still in front of me."

May your greatest achievements be in front of you and may you always Finish Strong.

"EFFORT ONLY FULLY RELEASES ITS REWARD AFTER A PERSON REFUSES TO QUIT"

— NAPOLEON HILL

ABOUT THE AUTHOR

Dan is an entrepreneur with a passion for finishing strong in everything he does. Over the past 20 years, he has excelled in his roles as salesman, sales leader, sales trainer, patented inventor, race car driver, author, speaker, husband and father. Adopting the "Finish Strong" attitude has been a driving force in Dan's life and a key catalyst in achieving his goals in business, sports and in life. He currently serves as a partner and Executive Vice President with Simple Truths and is the founder of Finish Strong, LLC.

Dan is the author of three inspirational books; *Finish Strong, Finish Strong Teen Athlete* and *Finish Strong Motivational Quotes*. Collectively his books have been purchased by more than 250,000 people across the globe. The first *Finish Strong* book was used by Drew Brees and the New Orleans Saints as a guiding theme on the way to their Super Bowl victory.

Since receiving the trademark rights to the words "Finish Strong" in 1996, Dan has been the evangelist for incorporating its message of challenge and inspiration in every aspect of life. During this time, thousands of people from all walks of life have adopted the Finish Strong attitude in their lives; ultimately beating the odds to overcome adversity and achieve their dreams.

For more information about Dan, to inquire about speaking engagements, or to learn more about incorporating Finish Strong into your next event, send an email to Contact@finishstrong.com or visit:

WWW.FINISHSTRONG.COM

I have fought a good fight.
I have finished the race,
I have kept the faith.

[2 TIMOTHY 4:7]

The
simple truths®
DIFFERENCE

If you have enjoyed this book we invite you to check out our entire collection of gift books and free inspirational movies, at **www.simpletruths.com.**

You'll discover it's a great way to inspire *friends* and *family,* or to thank your best *customers* and *employees.*

There is one thing in life that took me a long time to learn, and that's ... less is almost always more. This "simple truth" is the foundation on which our company was built. I wanted to create beautiful gift books that anyone can read in less than thirty minutes.

To make each book special, we focused on three things:
1. Great content
2. Great graphics
3. Great packaging to create a *"wow effect"*

Satisfied customers are our #1 priority, so I encourage you to give us feedback on how we're doing. If we ever disappoint you, I hope you'll let us know, and we will do everything we can to make it right. Please send your comments to:

Simple Truths Feedback
P.O. Box 4410, Naperville, Illinois 60567-4410
(630) 961-3900

E-mails us at: *comments@simpletruths.com*

or call toll free ... *800-900-3427*